His Hands Were Gentle
Selected Lyrics of Víctor Jara

His Hands Were Gentle
Selected Lyrics of Víctor Jara
Edited by Martín Espada

First published 2012 by Smokestack Books
1 Lake Terrace, Grewelthorpe, Ripon, North Yorkshire HG4 3BU
e-mail: info@smokestack-books.co.uk
www.smokestack-books.co.uk

His Hands Were Gentle: Selected Lyrics of Víctor Jara
Edited by Martín Espada

Spanish text copyright Joan Jara and Amanda Jara.
English translations copyright Eduardo Embry, Martín Espada, John Green, Joan Jara and Celia Mitchell.

Foreword copyright Joan Jara
Preface copyright Emma Thompson
Introduction copyright Martín Espada
'Víctor Jara of Chile' copyright Celia Mitchell

ISBN 978-0-9568144-1-8

Smokestack Books is
represented by Inpress Ltd
www.inpressbooks.co.uk

To the memory of
Víctor Jara (1932-73) and Adrian Mitchell (1932-2008)

Indice

- 8 Prólogo por Joan Jara
- 11 Prefacio por Emma Thompson
- 12 Introducción por Martín Espada

- 17 Víctor Jara of Chile por Adrian Mitchell

- 20 Canción del minero
- 22 La luna siempre es muy linda
- 24 ¿Qué saco rogar al cielo?
- 26 El carretero
- 28 El arado
- 30 En algún lugar del puerto
- 32 El pimiento
- 34 La pala
- 36 El aparecido
- 38 Te recuerdo, Amanda
- 40 Plegaría a un labrador
- 44 Preguntas por Puerto Montt
- 48 A Luis Emilio Recabarren
- 50 Angelita Huenumán
- 54 Canto libre
- 56 El alma llena de banderas
- 58 Ni chicha ni limoná
- 62 Abre la ventana
- 64 Caminando, caminando
- 66 Lo único que tengo
- 68 El hombre es un creador
- 70 Manifiesto
- 72 Cuando voy al trabajo
- 76 Estadio Chile

- 80 Notas
- 82 Lectura
- 83 Los Traductores

Contents

- 8   Foreword by Joan Jara
- 11 Preface by Emma Thompson
- 12 Introduction by Martín Espada

- 17 Víctor Jara of Chile by Adrian Mitchell

- 21 Miner's Song
- 23 The Moon is Always Beautiful
- 25 Why Should I Pray to Heaven?
- 27 The Carter
- 29 The Plough
- 31 Somewhere in Valparaíso
- 33 The Pimiento Tree
- 35 The Spade
- 37 Apparition
- 39 I Remember You, Amanda
- 41 Prayer to a Labourer
- 45 Questions about the Massacre of Puerto Montt
- 49 For Luis Emilio Recabarren
- 51 Angelita Huenumán
- 55 Free Song
- 57 Our Hearts are Full of Banners
- 59 Don't Know, Don't Act
- 63 Open the Window
- 65 I Walk, I Walk
- 67 The Only Thing I Have
- 69 Man is a Creator
- 71 Manifesto
- 73 On My Way to Work
- 77 Chile Stadium

- 80 Notes
- 82 Further Reading
- 83 The Translators

Foreword

On 28 September 2012 we shall celebrate Víctor's birthday as we have done every year since his torture and murder by members of the Chilean armed forces almost forty years ago, in the Stadium which now bears his name.

It will be eighty years since Víctor was born. In his short life the barefooted peasant boy became a distinguished, prize-winning theatre director whose work was known beyond the borders of his own country. But it is not for this that Víctor is remembered today.

As a child living in the countryside it was natural for Víctor to absorb the traditional music and poetry of Chilean folklore. Although he never had any formal musical education, song was a natural form of expression for him. When he started instinctively to compose his own songs, they were a necessity surging from his own life experience, as true testimonies of real people, of love, of hope, and above all of the struggle for social justice during the turbulent years in which he lived and died.

He never forgot his origins and the deprived people among whom he spent his youth. His life-long commitment to fight for social justice was born in the sordid, poverty-stricken districts of Santiago where he lived as an adolescent.

After the brutal military coup of 11 September 1973, Víctor's songs became part of a clandestine resistance movement reaching out from an isolated and remote country to the rest of the world. In some strange way they crossed frontiers of language and cultures and Víctor's voice continued to be heard, singing as part of the enormous wave of international solidarity with the people of Chile.

Long years have passed. If Víctor lived only half his life I have lived two. The first ended as I stood before his tortured, bullet-ridden body in the city morgue in Santiago.

The second began painfully and slowly as, with my two beloved daughters, I arrived in London to begin our exile as refugees.

We were so lucky. Poet Adrian Mitchell and his wife Celia, opened their home to us although we were strangers to them and while Celia organised my daughters into local schools, I had long conversations with Adrian about Víctor, his life, his death and his songs. Adrian was gentle and sensitive. Being able to talk to him about Víctor began a healing process which gradually brought me back to life. Out of these conversations emerged many of the English versions of Víctor's lyrics which are in this book.

Little news of what was really happening in Chile was published in Britain in those first months after the coup. The British government was anxious to recognize the military junta. But we received messages about friends who had been arrested, killed or who had simply disappeared. As I began to receive invitation after invitation to attend memorial concerts for Víctor or to speak at solidarity meetings in different countries I realised that I had very strong motivation to start my second life. So different from the first. Apart from my never abandoned responsibility for my daughters, my task was to enable Víctor to fight back against the criminals who were ruling Chile, killing and torturing so many innocent people. I would try to keep alive his values, his voice, his songs and the memory of his dedicated life.

I have received so much solidarity, so much love and kindness from people in different countries of the world who were strangers to me but who became life-long friends. Thank you Adrian and Celia, thank you Peggy, Frances, Nat, Stanley, Martín, Mike, Liz, Diane, Pete and Toshi, Jeannie, Mavis, Emma, Peter – the list is endless.

Today in Chile we have not yet achieved the 'Truth and Justice' which the families of so many victims yearn for. The majority of the criminals hide behind the protective secrecy of the Armed Forces. Even though the case of Víctor has been called 'emblematic', the officers responsible for his assassination have never been identified.

Nevertheless, Víctor has received another kind of justice. The brave young people who are marching on the streets of Chile for a better future – they remember him.

Joan Jara
Santiago

Preface

When the Twin Towers were destroyed on September 11th 2001 I was in Scotland with my family. We had no television and listened only on the radio. In the midst of the appalled disbelief, I was keenly aware of another tragic relationship with that date. 11 September 1973 was the day a military dictatorship, led by Augusto Pinochet, executed a coup on the democratically elected Socialist government of Salvador Allende, a coup that resulted in thousands of deaths.

Of the innocents who suffered torture and murder at the hands of the junta, one was Víctor Jara. I had already been to Chile twice on the trail of his story, trying to write a biopic about his life. I failed to get a film made but I received an extraordinary education about Víctor, his family and his country.

For me, Víctor was everything an activist-musician should be. The music was central, politics were – unfortunately – necessary and fame was embarrassment.

He meant this to me: if you see something very wrong, then do something about it. Say something, sing something, write something. You can't stay silent. Speak about it with, above all, compassion and humour. Do anything you can, big or small, except stand back with your hands raised, disclaiming responsibility.

He was one of the most important influences on my young mind and I shall always be grateful to him and always honour him.

Emma Thompson
London

Introduction

In 1977, at the age of twenty, in Madison, Wisconsin, I attended a concert by the Chilean folk ensemble Inti-Illimani. In the middle of the concert, a banner unfurled onstage. The banner said: *Víctor Jara – ¡Presente!* The crowd exploded. I was baffled; I had never heard of Víctor Jara. He would soon become one of the most important voices in my life as a poet and activist.

Víctor Jara was born in 1932 in the village of Lonquén, fifty miles from Santiago de Chile. His father, Manuel Jara, an illiterate farm-labourer, abandoned the family when Víctor was very young. Víctor's mother, Amanda Martínez, raised him and his siblings. A well-known local singer, she died when Víctor was fifteen.

After two years in the seminary followed by a year in the army (where, ironically, he received high marks), Víctor studied drama at the University of Chile. Throughout the 1960s Víctor worked as a theatre director in Santiago, directing classics by Sophocles and Brecht, as well as contemporary works by the likes of Joe Orton and the Chilean Alejandro Sieveking.

All along Víctor was collecting, writing and performing songs, first with the folk-group Cuncumén, then with Quilapayún. He found himself at the vanguard of a movement: *La Nueva Canción Chilena* (Chilean New Song). In 1969, at Estadio Chile, backed by Quilapayún, Víctor won First Prize at the Festival of Chilean New Song for 'Plegaría a un labrador' (Prayer to a Labourer), which ends:

> We'll go together,
> united by blood,
> now and in the hour
> of our death. Amen.
> Amen.
> Amen.

The words were prophetic. Víctor sang this song in the same arena where he was murdered four years later.

Víctor was extraordinarily productive during his brief career: between 1966 and 1973 he released eight albums, including *Pongo en tus manos abiertas (I Put Into Your Open Hands), Canto Libre (Free Song)* and *El derecho de vivir en paz (The Right to Live in Peace)*. He toured throughout the world.

A committed and visible member of the Communist Party, Víctor performed all over Chile in support of socialist Salvador Allende's 1970 presidential campaign. His song, 'Venceremos' ('We will Win'), became an anthem for Allende, who prevailed at the polls, becoming the first democratically elected Marxist president in the Western Hemisphere.

However, his *Unidad Popular* (Popular Unity) government was destabilised by the Nixon White House, the CIA, the Henry Kissinger-chaired 'Forty Committee,' various US corporations, and the Chilean right wing. In response to this orchestration of political and economic sabotage and increasing acts of terror, Víctor spoke out. He sang at huge demonstrations in defence of Popular Unity. He directed a television series on the history of fascism, citing Nazi Germany and Franco's triumph in the Spanish Civil War, as a warning against the threat of fascism in Chile.

On 11 September 1973 the Chilean armed forces, with the support of the United States, overthrew the Popular Unity government. La Moneda, the Presidential Palace, was bombed; Allende died there after giving one final radio address to the nation. The following day Víctor was arrested at the Technical University and taken to Chile Stadium, one of 5,000 interned there in the days after the coup. He was beaten and tortured; the bones in both hands were broken. He was killed by the military on 16 September, shot 44 times.

During the seventeen-year dictatorship of General Augusto Pinochet that followed the coup, more 3,000 people were killed and at least 40,000 were imprisoned and tortured. Thousands more went into exile. It was Kissinger who infamously said of Chile: 'I don't see why we need to stand by and watch a country go communist due to the irresponsibility of its people.' Mrs Thatcher later thanked Pinochet 'for bringing democracy to Chile'.

Although Víctor's master tapes were destroyed, and his recordings were banned in Chile for many years, his compañera Joan Jara smuggled some recordings out of the country, which were then copied and distributed. In New York, Phil Ochs organized a concert in memory of Víctor, Allende and democratic Chile, featuring performances by Bob Dylan, Pete Seeger, Arlo Guthrie and Dennis Hopper. In East Germany, Dean Reed directed and starred in a biopic about Víctor. In the Soviet Union there was a rock opera about Víctor's death. His life and work have influenced musicians such as U2, Christy Moore, Simple Minds and The Clash. As Pete Seeger put it, 'as long as we sing his songs, as long as his courage can inspire us to greater courage, Víctor Jara will never die.'

Today Víctor's music resonates far beyond the borders of Chile, thanks in great part to the work of Joan Jara and her Víctor Jara Foundation. However, outside the Spanish-speaking world the lyrics themselves do not receive the attention they deserve. *His Hands Were Gentle* brings together, for the first time in both Spanish and English, the most beautiful and powerful of Víctor Jara's lyrics, from early songs like 'La luna siempre es muy linda' ('The Moon is Always Very Beautiful') to 'Estadio Chile' ('Chile Stadium'), written in the hours before his death. They show him as an ardent political poet, an eloquent advocate for the peasantry from which he arose, a socialist visionary and a poetic balladeer of the highest order.

Translation of song lyrics, of course, is not quite the same process as the translation of poetry. Issues of fidelity and creativity take on even greater urgency.

It is not a comprehensive selection. One on-line database credits Víctor with more than 150 songs. Not all the lyrics are equally 'translatable' to the page. Not all the lyrics were written by him. He was particularly accomplished at setting poetry to music, and, in fact, some of his most renowned songs involve sensitive renderings of poetry by such masters as Miguel Hernández, Nicolás Guillén and Víctor's friend Pablo Neruda. (Upon hearing of Víctor's murder, Neruda, himself on his deathbed, said: 'Oh my God, it's like killing a nightingale.')

Chile celebrated the centenary of Neruda in July 2004. I was invited with a U.S. delegation to participate in the celebration. Víctor's music was everywhere. In Santiago I met Joan Jara, and travelled with her to the place where Víctor was assassinated, now renamed 'Estadio Víctor Jara' in his memory. There, I read her a poem dedicated to Víctor by the Jamaican writer Andrew Salkey, one of my mentors, calling upon all of us to:

> Love the words he used;
> clasp the poetry close;
> wrap the strings tight;
> sing all his songs, again!

That is the spirit of the book you hold in your hand.

Martín Espada
Amherst, Massachusetts

Víctor Jara of Chile

Víctor Jara of Chile
Lived like a shooting star
He fought for the people of Chile
With his songs and his guitar
And his hands were gentle,
His hands were strong.

Víctor Jara was a peasant
He worked from a few years old
He sat upon his father's plough
And watched the earth unfold
And his hands were gentle
His hands were strong.

Now when the neighbours had a wedding
Or one of their children died
His mother sang all night for them
With Víctor by her side
And his hands were gentle
His hands were strong.

He grew up to be a fighter
Against the people's wrongs
He listened to their grief and joy
And turned them into songs
And his hands were gentle
His hands were strong.

He sang about the copper miners
And those who worked the land
He sang about the factory workers
And they knew he was their man
And his hands were gentle
His hands were strong.

He campaigned for Allende
Working night and day
He sang: Take hold of your brother's hand
You know the future begins today
And his hands were gentle
His hands were strong.

The bloody generals seized Chile
They arrested Víctor then
They caged him in a stadium
With five-thousand frightened men
And his hands were gentle
His hands were strong.

Víctor stood in the stadium
His voice was brave and strong
And he sang for his fellow prisoners
Till the guards cut short his song
And his hands were gentle
His hands were strong.

They broke the bones in both his hands
They beat his lovely head
They tore him with electric shocks
After two long days of torture they shot him dead
And his hands were gentle
His hands were strong.

And now the Generals rule Chile
And the British have their thanks
For they rule with Hawker Hunters
And they rule with Chieftain tanks
And his hands were gentle
His hands were strong.

Víctor Jara of Chile
Lived like a shooting star
He fought for the people of Chile
With his songs and his guitar
And his hands were gentle
His hands were strong.

Adrian Mitchell

Canción del minero

Voy, vengo, subo, bajo,
todo para qué,
nada para mí.
Minero soy,
a la mina voy,
a la muerte voy,
minero soy.

Abro, saco, sudo, sangro,
todo pa'l patron,
nada pa'l dolor.
Minero soy,
a la mina voy,
a la muerte voy,
minero soy.

Mira, oye, piensa, grita,
nada es lo peor,
todo es lo mejor.
Minero soy,
a la mina voy,
a la muerte voy,
minero soy.

(1961)

Miner's Song

Coming, going, crawling,
all for what?
Nothing is for me.
A miner I am,
to the mine I go,
to death I go,
a miner I am.

Digging, dragging, sweating, bleeding,
all for the Boss
nothing for my pain.
A miner I am,
to the mine I go,
to death I go,
a miner I am.

Watch, listen, reason, shout,
nothing could be worse,
anything is better
A miner I am,
to the mine I go,
to death I go,
a miner I am.

translated by Joan Jara

La luna siempre es muy linda

Recuerdo el rostro de mi padre
como un hueco en la muralla,
sábanas manchadas de barro,
piso de tierra,
mi madre día y noche trabajando,
llantos y gritos.

Jugando al ángel y al diablo,
jugando al hijo que no va a nacer,
las velas siempre encendidas,
hay que refugiarse en algo,
¿de dónde sale el dinero
para pagar la fe?

No recuerdo que desde el cielo
haya bajado una cosecha gloriosa,
ni que mi madre hubiera tenido un poco de paz,
ni que mi padre hubiera dejado de beber.

Al pobre tanto lo asustan
para que trague todos sus dolores,
para que su miseria la cubra de imágenes.
La luna siempre es muy linda
y el sol muere cada tarde.

Por eso quiero gritar:
no creo en nada
sino en el calor
de tu mano con mi mano.
Por eso quiero gritar:
no creo en nada
sino en el amor
de los seres humanos.

¿Quién puede callar el latido
de un corazón palpitando
o el grito de una mujer dando un hijo?
¿Quién?

(1962)

The Moon is Always Beautiful

I remember the face of my father
as a hole in the wall,
mud-stained sheets,
an earthen floor,
my mother working day and night,
weeping and shouting.

Playing at angels and devils,
playing at the child who will never be born,
candles always burning,
one must take refuge in something,
where will the money come from
to pay for faith?

I can't remember that a glorious harvest
has ever descended from heaven
or that my mother ever had a little peace,
or that my father ever stopped drinking.

They frighten the poor so much
so that they will swallow their suffering,
so that they will cover their misery with images of saints.
The moon is always beautiful,
the sun dies every evening.

And that is why I want to shout:
I believe in nothing
but the warmth
of your hand in mine.
I want to shout:
I believe in nothing
but the love
of human beings.

Who can silence the pulse
of a beating heart
or the cry of a woman giving birth to a child?
Who?

translated by Joan Jara

¿Qué saco rogar al cielo?

¿Qué saco rogar al cielo
si en tierra me han de enterrar?
La tierra me da comía,
la tierra me hace sudar.

Qué saco sudando tanto
y comiendo poco y ná,
si mi tierra no es mi tierra
y el cielo, cielo no más.

Adonde pongo mis manos
brotan claveles y rosas,
brotan y brotan las cosas
que no aprovecha mi mano.

Una espiga hay en el campo,
una espiga colorá,
si juntos la cosechamos
grande será nuestro pan.

(1962)

Why Should I Pray to Heaven?

Why should I pray to heaven
when I will be buried in the earth?
The earth gives me food,
the earth makes me sweat.

Why should I sweat so much
eating little or nothing
if my land is not my land
and the sky is only sky.

Wherever I lay my hands,
carnations and roses flower,
things which I cannot use
grow and grow.

An ear of corn ripens in the countryside,
a red ear of corn,
if we harvest it together
our bread will be plentiful.

translated by Joan Jara

El carretero

Por un camino 'e trumao
va la carreta crujiendo,
palpita la ventolera
entre las hojas del trébol.

Mi vida es sólo trumao,
ventoleras y silencio,
camino el mismo camino,
con mi yunta voy y vengo.

La tarde baila en las nubes,
cubre de sangre los cerros,
una corona de buitres
acompaña al carretero.

A veces pierdo la huella
mientras el corazón da un vuelco.
¿Cuándo mi vida tendrá
el camino que yo quiero?

Un aleteo de sombras
alarga más el silencio,
como hundiéndose en la noche
la carreta va crujiendo.

Yo también abro la tierra
y con ella abro mi fe.
¡Apúrate, yunta 'e negro',
que comienza a amanecer!

(1964)

The Carter

On the stony-track
the cart creaks,
gusts of wind
blow through the clover leaves.

My life consists of pumice-stone,
wind and silence,
I always tread the same road
and with my oxen I come and go.

The afternoon dances in the clouds,
blood drenches the mountains,
a crown of vultures
accompany the carter.

Now and again I lose the track
and my heart misses a beat.
When will my life take
the path I want?

A wingbeat of shadows
deepens the silence,
as if the night had sunk away
the cart creaks on its way.

I, too, open the earth
and let my faith grow.
Come on, you oxen
It will soon be dawn!

translated by Eduardo Embry and John Green

El arado

Aprieto firme mi mano
y hundo el arado en la tierra,
hace años que llevo en ella,
cómo no estar agotao.

Vuelan mariposas, cantan grillos,
la piel se me pone negra
y el sol brilla, brilla y brilla.
El sudor me hace surcos,
yo hago surcos a la tierra
sin parar.

Afirmo bien la esperanza
cuando pienso en la otra estrella,
nunca es tarde me dice ella,
la paloma volará.

Vuelan mariposas, cantan grillos,
la piel se me pone negra
y el sol brilla, brilla y brilla.
Y en la tarde cuando vuelvo,
en el cielo, apareciendo,
una estrella.

Nunca es tarde me dice ella,
la paloma volará, volará, volará.
Como yugo de apretao,
tengo el puño esperanzao,
porque todo cambiará.

(1965)

The Plough

I clench my fist
and bury the plough in the earth,
for years and years I have worked,
no wonder I am worn out.

Butterflies are flying, crickets are singing,
my skin gets darker and darker,
and the sun glares, glares and glares.
Sweat furrows me,
I make furrows in the earth,
on and on.

I hold fast to hope
when I think of my other star.
'It is never too late,' she tells me,
'the dove will fly one day.'

Butterflies are flying, crickets are singing,
my skin gets darker and darker
and the sun glares, glares and glares.
And in the evening going home
in the sky I see
a star.

'It is never too late,' she tells me,
'the dove will fly one day.'
As tight as a yoke
my fist is full of hope
because everything will change.

translated by Adrian Mitchell

En algún lugar del puerto

Voy soñando, voy caminando, voy.
En la arena dejo mis huellas, voy.
Y el mar me las va borrando, voy.

El viento sube a los cerros,
con el viento mis recuerdos,
corriendo al cerro El Aromo,
pelota de trapo al cielo,
corriendo vuelvo a la casa,
mi madre siempre cosiendo,
mi padre ¿dónde estará?

El viejo era pescador,
sencillo como sus remos,
para existir mar afuera
trabajaba mar adentro.

El mar le ofrecía todo
entregándosele quieto
y el mar le quitó la vida
con su remolina negro.

Un grito agudo del viento
atraviesa por los cerros
¿dónde se fueron mis hijos?
¿Cuántos desaparecieron?

Voy soñando, voy caminando, voy.
En la arena dejo mis huellas, voy.
Y el mar me las va borrando, voy.

(1965)

Somewhere in Valparaíso

I walk dreamily, wander and wander
leaving tracks in the sand, walking
and the sea washes them away again and again.

The wind rises over the hills,
and with the wind my memories,
running over to El Amorro hill,
with my ball made of rags that sails to the skies,
running, I return home,
my mother silently cooking,
and my father, where could he be?

My old man was a fisherman,
ordinary as his oars,
in order to live onshore
he had to work far out to sea.

The sea provided everything
when it lay calm
and the sea took his life
with its dark eddies.

Shrill cry of the wind
through the hills,
Where have my children gone?
How many have disappeared?

I walk dreamily, wander and wander
leaving tracks in the sand, walking,
and the sea washes them away again and again.

translated by Eduardo Embry and John Green

El pimiento

En el centro de la pampa
vive un pimiento,
sol y viento pa' su vida,
sol y viento.

Coronado por la piedra
vive el pimiento,
luna y viento lo vigilan,
luna y viento.

Cuando sus ramas florecen
es un incendio,
tanto rojo que derraman,
rojo entero,
rojo entero.

Nadie lo ve trabajar
debajo el suelo,
cuando busca noche y día
su alimento.

Pimiento rojo del norte
atacameño,
siento el canto de tus ramas
en el desierto.

Debes seguir floreciendo
como un incendio,
porque el norte es todo tuyo,
todo entero,
todo entero.

(1965)

The Pimiento Tree

In the centre of the desert
there is a pimiento tree,
sun and wind give it life,
sun and wind.

Crowned with stone
lives the pimiento tree,
moon and wind watch over it,
moon and wind.

When its branches flower
it is ablaze with fire,
it overflows with red,
red all over,
red all over.

Nobody sees it working
beneath the ground,
while night and day
it seeks its nourishment.

Red pimiento tree of the north
of Atacama,
I can hear the song of your branches
in the desert.

You must go on flowering
ablaze with fire
because all the north belongs to you,
to you alone,
to you alone.

translated by Joan Jara

La pala

Me entregaron una pala
que la cuidara pa' mí,
que nunca la abandonara
pa' que la tierra regara,
despacito, despacito.

Y cuando más mocetón
me entregaron un arado,
que lo empujara con fuerza
pa' que gritara la tierra,
despacito, despacito.

Llévalos por los caminos
como llevas tu destino.
El trabajo hay que cuidar,
ellos te darán el pan.
Llévalos por los caminos.

Enyugado por los años,
mi cuero ya no es más,
todo lo trabajao,
toito me lo han quitao,
despacito, despacito.

Malhaya la vida oscura
que he tenío que llevar,
pero he visto que la noche
ha comenzao a aclarar,
despacito, despacito.

Sigue abriendo en los caminos
el surco de tu destino.
La alegría de sembrar
no te la puden quitar,
la alegría de sembrar
es tuya, de nadie más.

(1967)

The Spade

They gave me a spade
that I was to look after,
so I would never leave,
so I would dig the soil
slowly, very slowly.

When I was older
they gave me a plough,
that I was to steer manfully
until the earth cried out,
slowly, very slowly.

Take them on your journeys
as you take your own fate.
Work needs to be cherished,
it will give you your bread.
Take them on your journeys.

Yoked by the years,
my body can give no more,
everything I worked for,
they took it all away
slowly, very slowly.

I curse the dark life
I have had to bear,
but I have seen that the darkness
has started to lift,
slowly, very slowly.

Carry on ploughing open
the roads of your destiny
the joy of sowing
no one can take from you
the joy of sowing
is yours, yours alone.

translated by Eduardo Embry and John Green

El aparecido

dedicada a Ché Guevara

Abre sendas por los cerros,
deja su huella en el viento,
el águila le da el vuelo
y lo cobija el silencio.

Nunca se quejó del frío,
nunca se quejó del sueño,
el pobre siente su paso
y lo sigue como ciego.

Correlé, correlé, correlá,
por aquí, por allí, por allá,
correlé, correlé, correlá,
correlé que te van a matar,
correlé, correlé, correlá.

Su cabeza es rematada
por cuervos con garras de oro,
cómo lo ha crucificado
la furia del poderoso.

Hijo de la rebeldía,
lo siguen veinte más veinte,
porque regala su vida
ellos le quieren dar muerte.

Correlé, correlé, correlá,
por aquí, por allí, por allá,
correlé, correlé, correlá,
correlé que te van a matar,
correlé, correlé, correlá.

(1967)

Apparition

for Ché Guevara

He finds paths among the mountains,
leaves his footprint on the wind,
the eagle gives him flight
and the silence shelters him.

He never complains of cold,
never complains of fatigue,
the poor hear his passing
and blindly follow him.

Fly, fly, hide,
here, there, everywhere,
fly, fly, hide,
fly, because they will kill you,
fly, fly, hide.

The vultures with golden claws
have put their price upon his head,
the fury of the powerful
will crucify him.

Son of the revolution,
followed by twenty and twenty,
because his life is dedicated
they want to murder him.

Fly, fly, hide,
here, there, everywhere,
fly, fly, hide,
fly, because they will kill you,
fly, fly, hide.

translated by Joan Jara

Te recuerdo, Amanda

Te recuerdo Amanda,
la calle mojada,
corriendo a la fábrica
donde trabajaba Manuel.

La sonrisa ancha,
la lluvia en el pelo,
no importaba nada,
ibas a encontrarte con él,
con él, con él, con él, con él,
son cinco minutos,
la vida es eterna
en cinco minutos.

Suena la sirena,
de vuelta al trabajo
y tú, caminando,
lo iluminas todo,
los cinco minutos
te hacen florecer.

Que partió a la sierra,
que nunca hizo daño,
que partió a la sierra
y en cinco minutos
quedó destrozado.

Suena la sirena,
de vuelta al trabajo,
muchos no volvieron,
tampoco Manuel.

Te recuerdo Amanda,
la calle mojada,
corriendo a la fábrica
donde trabajaba Manuel.

(1968)

I Remember You, Amanda

I remember you Amanda,
when the streets were wet,
running to the factory
where Manuel was working.

With your wide smile,
the rain in your hair,
nothing else mattered,
you were going to meet him,
with him, with him, with him, with him,
five minutes only,
all of your life
in five minutes.

The siren sounding,
time to go back to work.
And as you walk
you light up everything,
those five minutes
have made you flower.

And he took to the mountains to fight,
he had never hurt a fly,
he took to the mountains
and in five minutes
it was all wiped out.

The siren sounding,
time to go back to work,
many will not go back,
one of them is Manuel.

I remember you Amanda,
when the streets were wet,
running to the factory
where Manuel was working.

translated by Adrian Mitchell

Plegaría a un labrador

Levántate
y mira la montaña,
de donde viene
el viento, el sol y el agua.
Tú que manejas
el curso do los ríos,
tú que sembraste
el vuelo de tu alma.

Levántate
y mírate las manos,
para crecer
estréchala a tu hermano,
juntos iremos
unidos en la sangre,
hoy es el tiempo
que puede ser mañana.

Líbranos de aquel que nos domina
en la miseria,
tráenos tu reino de justicia
e igualdad.

Sopla como el viento
la flor de la quebrada,
limpia como el fuego
el cañón de mi fusil.

Hágase por fin tu voluntad
aquí en la tierra,
danos tu fuerza y tu valor
al combatir.

Sopla como el viento
la flor de la quebrada,
limpia como el fuego
el cañón de mi fusil.

Prayer to a Labourer

Stand up
look at the mountain,
source
of the wind, the sun, the water.
You who change
the course of rivers,
who with the seed sows
the flight of your soul.

Stand up
look at your hands,
take your brother's hand
so you can grow,
we'll go together,
united by blood,
the future
can begin today.

Deliver us from the master who keeps us
in misery,
thy will be done, at last,
on earth.

Blow like the wind blows
the wild flower of the mountain pass,
clean the barrel of my gun
like fire.

Thy will be done, at last,
on earth,
give us the strength and courage
to struggle.

Blow like the wind blows
the wild flower of the mountain pass,
clean the barrel of my gun
like fire.

Levántate
y mírate las manos,
para crecer
estréchala a tu hermano,
juntos iremos
unidos en la sangre,
ahora y en la hora
de nuestra muerte, amén.
Amén.
Amén.

(1969)

Stand up
look at your hands,
take your brother's hand
so you can grow,
we'll go together,
united by blood,
now and in the hour
of our death. Amen.
Amen.
Amen.

translated by Adrian Mitchell

Preguntas por Puerto Montt

Muy bien, voy a preguntar
por ti, por ti, por aquel,
por ti que quedaste solo
y el que murió sin saber.

Muy bien, voy a preguntar
por ti, por ti, por aquel,
por ti que quedaste solo
y el que murió sin saber,
que murió sin saber.

Murió sin saber porqué
le acribillaban el pecho
luchando por el derecho
de un suelo para vivir.
¡Ay! Qué ser más infeliz,
el que mandó a disparar,
sabiendo como evitar
una matanza tan vil.

¡Puerto Montt, oh Puerto Montt!
¡Puerto Montt, oh Puerto Montt!
¡Puerto Montt, oh Puerto Montt!
¡Puerto Montt, oh Puerto Montt!

Usted debe responder,
señor Pérez Zujovic,
por qué al pueblo indefenso
contestaron con fusil.

Señor Pérez, su conciencia
la enterró en un ataúd
y no limpiará sus manos
toda la lluvia del sur,
toda la lluvia del sur.

Questions about the Massacre of Puerto Montt

Very well, I will ask
for you, for you, for him,
for you left all alone, for the man
who died and never knew why.

Very well, I will ask
for you, for you, for him,
for you left all alone, for the man
who died and never knew why,
died and never knew why.

He died and never knew why
the bullets riddled his chest
when he fought for the right
to a place to live on this earth.
What kind of miserable creature
gives the order to fire
knowing he could avoid
a massacre so vile?

Puerto Montt, oh Puerto Montt!
Puerto Montt, oh Puerto Montt!
Puerto Montt, oh Puerto Montt!
Puerto Montt, oh Puerto Montt!

And you must tell us,
Mr. Pérez Zujovic,
why you answered
defenceless people with gunfire.

Mr. Pérez, you've buried
your conscience In a coffin,
and you cannot wash your hands
with all the rains of the south,
all the rains of the south.

Murió sin saber porqué
le acribillaban el pecho
luchando por el derecho
de un suelo para vivir.
¡Ay! Qué ser más infeliz,
el que mandó a disparar,
sabiendo como evitar
una matanza tan vil.

¡Puerto Montt, oh Puerto Montt!
¡Puerto Montt, oh Puerto Montt!
¡Puerto Montt, oh Puerto Montt!
¡Puerto Montt, oh Puerto Montt!

(1969)

He died and never knew why
the bullets riddled his chest
when he fought for the right
to a place to live on this earth.
What kind of miserable creature
gives the order to fire
knowing he could avoid
a massacre so vile?

Puerto Montt, oh Puerto Montt!
Puerto Montt, oh Puerto Montt!
Puerto Montt, oh Puerto Montt!
Puerto Montt, oh Puerto Montt!

Translated by Martín Espada

A Luis Emilio Recabarren

Pongo en tus manos abiertas
mi guitarra de cantor,
martillo de los mineros,
arado del labrador.

Recabarren,
Luis Emilio Recabarren,
simplemente
doy las gracias por tu luz.
Con el viento,
con el viento de la pampa,
tu voz sopla
por el centro y por el sur.

Árbol de tanta esperanza,
naciste en medio del sol,
tu fruto madura y canta
hacia la liberación.

Recabarren,
Luis Emilio Recabarren,
simplemente
doy las gracias por tu luz.
Con el viento,
con el viento de la pampa,
tu voz sopla
por el centro y por el sur.

(1969)

For Luis Emilio Recabarren

I place in your open hands
my singer's guitar,
the miners' hammer,
the peasant's plough.

Recabarren,
Luis Emilio Recabarren,
I say, simply,
thank you for your light.
On the wind,
on the wind of the Pampas,
your voice is carried
to the centre and to the south.

Tree of so much hope,
born in the sunlight,
your fruit will ripen and sing
until we are free.

Recabarren,
Luis Emilio Recabarren,
I say, simply,
thank you for your light.
On the wind,
on the wind of the Pampas,
your voice is carried
to the centre and to the south.

translated by Eduardo Embry and John Green

Angelita Huenumán

En la valle de Pocuno,
donde rebota el viento del mar,
donde la lluvia cría a los musgos,
vive Angelita Huenumán.

Entre el mañío y los hualles,
el avellano y el pitrán,
entre el aroma de las chilcas,
vive Angelita Huenumán.

Cuidada por cinco perros,
un hijo que dejó el amor,
sencilla como su chacrita,
el mundo gira alrededor.

La sangre roja del copihue
corre en sus venas Huenumán,
junto a la luz de una ventana
teje Angelita su vida.

Sus manos bailan en la hebra
como alitas de chincol,
es un milagro como teje
hasta el aroma de la flor.

En tus telares, Angelita,
hay tiempo, lágrima y sudor,
están las manos ignoradas
de este, mi pueblo creador.

Después de meses de trabajo
el chamal busca comprador,
y como pájaro enjaulado
canta para el mejor postor.

Angelita Huenumán

In the valley of Pocuno
ruffled by the sea wind,
where the rain feeds the moss,
lives Angelita Huenumán.

Among the oak trees and the reeds,
among the hazel woods and the gorse,
in the aroma of wild fuschias,
lives Angelita Huenumán.

Taken care of by five dogs,
and a son left over from love,
as simple as her little farm,
the world revolves around her.

The red blood of the copihue flower
runs in her Huenemán veins,
by the light of the window
Angelita weaves her life.

Her hands dance in the hemp
like the wings of a little bird,
she weaves a flower so miraculously
that you can smell its perfume.

Angelita, in your weaving
there is time and tears and sweat,
there are the anonymous hands
of my creative people.

After months of work
the extraordinary blanket looks for a buyer
and like a bird in a cage
sings for the highest bidder.

Entre el mañío y los hualles,
el avellano y el pitrán,
entre el aroma de las chilcas,
vive Angelita Huenumán.

(1969)

Among the oak trees and the reeds
among the hazel woods and the gorse
in the aroma of wild fuschias
lives Angelita Huenumán.

translated by Adrian Mitchell

Canto libre

El verso es una paloma
que busca donde anidar,
estalla y abre sus alas
para volar y volar.

Mi canto es un canto libre
que se quiere regalar
a quien estreche su mano,
a quien quiera disparar.

Mi canto es una cadena
sin comienzo ni final,
y en cada eslabón se encuentra
el canto de los demás.

Sigamos cantando juntos
a toda la humanidad,
que el canto es una paloma
que vuela para alcanzar,
estalla y abre sus alas
para volar y volar.

Mi canto es un canto libre.

(1970)

Free Song

My verse is a dove
looking for a place to nest,
exploding, spreading its wings
to fly and fly and fly.

My song is a free song,
it wants to give itself
to anyone who holds out a hand,
to anyone who wants to soar.

My song is a chain
without beginning or end,
and in every link you'll find
the song of all the people.

Let's go out singing together
to everyone on earth.
sing that song is a dove
flying, reaching out,
exploding, spreading its wings
to fly and fly and fly.

My song is a free song.

translated by Joan Jara

El alma llena de banderas

homenaje a Miguel Angel Aguilera

Ahí, debajo de la tierra,
no estás dormido, hermano, compañero.
Tu corazón
oye brotar la primavera
que como tú soplando irá los vientos.

Ahí, enterrado cara al sol,
la nueva tierra cubre tu semilla,
la raíz
profunda se hundirá
y nacerá la flor del nuevo día.

A tus pies heridos llegarán,
las manos del humilde, llegarán
sembrando.
Tu muerte muchas vidas traerá,
que hacia donde tú ibas, marcharán
cantando.

Allí, donde se oculta el criminal
tu nombre brinda al rico muchos nombres.
Él que quemó tus alas al volar,
no apagará el fuego de los pobres.

Aquí hermano, aquí sobre la tierra,
el alma se nos llena de banderas
que avanzan
contra el miedo
avanzan
contra el miedo
¡Venceremos!
¡Venceremos!

(1970)

Our Hearts are Full of Banners

In memory of Miguel-Angel Aguilera

There, under the earth,
you are not asleep, my brother, my comrade.
Your heart
hears the spring buds opening
they will ride upon the winds like you.

Buried there with your face to the sun,
the fresh earth covers your seed,
the root
will burrow deeply
and the flower of the new day will be born.

To your wounded feet
the hands of the humble will come
to sow.
Your death will cause many lives
to march where you were going,
singing.

In the hiding place of rich murderers
your name will stand for many names.
The one who burnt your wings as you flew
cannot put out the fire of the poor.

Here, my brother, here upon the earth
our hearts are full of banners
and they advance
against fear
and they advance
against fear
¡Venceremos!
¡Venceremos!

translated by Adrian Mitchell

Ni chicha ni limoná

Arrímese más pa'acá,
aquí donde el sol calienta,
si usté ya está acostumbrao
a andar dando volteretas
y ningún daño le hará
estar donde las papas queman.

Usté no es ná,
no es chicha ni limoná,
se lo pasa manoseando,
caramba zamba, su dignidad.

La fiesta ya ha comenzao
y la cosa está que arde.
Usté que era el más quedao,
se quiere adueñar del baile,
total a los olfatillos
no hay olor que se les escape.

Usté no es ná,
no es chicha ni limoná,
se lo pasa manoseando,
caramba zamba, su dignidad.

Si queremos más fiestoca
primero hay que trabajar,
y tendremos pa' toitos
abrigo, pan y amistad.
Y si usted no está de acuerdo
es cuestión de usté no más:
la cosa va pa' delante
y no piensa recular.

Don't Know, Don't Act

Come warm up your blood down here
and all of your lukewarm virtue,
you've sat on the fence so long
some standing will hardly hurt you.
The action down here is hot
but maybe it won't convert you.
The action down here is hot
but maybe it won't convert you.

Don't know, don't act,
you're zero and that's a fact.
Since you're half-awake, half-baked,
disaster master, get off my back.

The people are just warming up.
the party we've just begun it.
The last one to join the dance,
you say you want to run it.
And everything that gets done,
you claim you're the one who's done it.
And everything that gets done,
you claim you're the one who's done it.

Don't know, don't act,
you're zero and that's a fact.
Since you're half-awake, half-baked,
disaster master, get off my back.

We all want to see good times
so we're working helter-skelter.
Soon everybody can share
in friendship and food and shelter.
Too bad if you've got your doubts.
Too bad if I seem to doubt you.
The people are moving on
and they can move on without you.

Usté no es ná,
no es chicha ni limoná,
se lo pasa manoseando,
caramba zamba, su dignidad.

Ya déjese de patillas,
venga a remediar su mal,
si aquí debajito 'el poncho
no tengo ningún puñal.
Y si sigue hociconeando,
le vamos a expropriar
las pistolas y la lengua
y toito lo demás.

Usté no es ná,
no es chicha ni limoná,
se lo pasa manoseando,
caramba zamba, su dignidad.

(1970)

Don't know, don't act,
you're zero and that's a fact.
Since you're half-awake, half-baked,
disaster master, get off my back.

Forget your problems for once,
we'll cure your sickness for life.
Forget your nightmares for once,
I never carry a knife.
But if you keep shouting the odds
as you sit up there on your fence,
we'll give your guns and your gear
to people who've got more sense.

Don't know, don't act,
you're zero and that's a fact.
Since you're half-awake, half-baked,
disaster master, get off my back.

translated by Adrian Mitchell

Abre la ventana

María,
abre la ventana
y deja que el sol alumbre
por todos los rincones de tu casa.

María,
mira hacia afuera,
nuestra vida no ha sido hecha
para rodearla de sombras y tristeza.

María, ya ves,
no basta nacer, crecer, amar
para encontrar
la felicidad.

Pasó lo más cruel,
ahora tus ojos se llenan de luz
y tus manos de miel,
tus manos de miel,
tus manos de miel.
María…

Tu risa brota
como la mañana brota en el jardín.
María…

(1970)

Open the Window

María,
open the window
and let the sun light up
every corner of your house.

Maria,
look outside,
our life has not been made
to be surrounded with shadows and sadness.

Maria, don't you see,
it's not enough to be born, to grow, to love
in order to find
happiness.

The worst is over,
now your eyes are full of light
and your hands of honey,
your hands of honey.
your hands of honey.
Maria…

Your smile blossoms
as the morning blossoms in a garden.
Maria…

translated by Joan Jara

Caminando, caminando

Caminando, caminando,
voy buscando libertad,
ojalá encuentre camino
para seguir caminando.

Es difícil encontrar
en la sombra claridad,
cuando el sol que nos alumbra
descolora la verdad.

Cuánto tiempo estoy llegando,
desde cuándo me habré ido,
cuánto tiempo caminando,
desde cuándo caminando.

(1970)

I Walk, I Walk

I walk, I walk
I'm going to search for freedom
I hope to find the way
to keep going.

It's difficult to find
light in the shade
if the sun that lights the way
changes the colour of truth.

How much time will I need to get there?
When did I leave?
How long have I been walking?
Since when have I been walking?

translated by Eduardo Embry and John Green

Lo único que tengo

Quién me iba a decir a mí,
cómo me iba a imaginar,
si yo no tengo un lugar
si yo no tengo un lugar
si yo no tengo un lugar
en la tierra.

Mis manos son lo único que tengo,
y mis manos son mi amor y mi sustento,
y mis manos son lo único que tengo,
son mi amor y mi sustento.

No hay casa donde llegar,
mi paire y mi maire están
más lejos de este barrial
más lejos de este barrial
más lejos de este barrial
que una estrella.

(1972)

The Only Thing I Have

Who would tell me,
how could I imagine,
if I have no home
if I have no home
if I have no place
on this earth.

And my hands are all I have,
and my hands are my love and my living,
and my hands are all I have,
they are my love and my living.

I've no home to go to,
no father or mother there
far away from this swamp
far away from this swamp
far away from this swamp
like a star.

translated by Eduardo Embry and John Green

El hombre es un creador

Igualito que otros tantos
de niño aprendí a sudar,
no conocí las escuelas
ni supe lo que es jugar.
Me sacaban de la cama
por la mañana temprano,
y al laito 'e mi papá
fui creciendo en el trabajo.

Con mi pura habilidad
me las di de carpintero,
de estucador y albañil,
de gásfiter y tornero.
¡Puchas! Qué sería bueno
haber tenido instrucción,
porque de todo elemento
el hombre es un creador.

Yo le levanto una casa
o le construyo un camino,
le pongo sabor al vino,
le saco humito a la fábrica,
voy al fondo de la tierra
y conquisto las alturas,
camino por las estrellas
y hago surco a la espesura.

Aprendí el vocabulario
del amo, dueño y patrón,
me mataron tantas veces
por levantarles la voz,
pero del suelo me paro
porque me prestan las manos,
porque ahora no estoy solo,
porque ahora somos tantos.

(1972)

Man is a Creator

Like lots of other children
I was taught to sweat,
I didn't know what school was,
didn't know how to play.
They dragged me out of bed
early every morning,
and alongside my Dad
I grew up as a worker.

Because I was pretty handy
I got by as a carpenter,
a plasterer and a brick-layer,
a plumber and a mechanic.
Hey! It would have been useful
to have had some sort of schooling,
that would have been one more thing to use –
Man as a creator.

I can build you a house,
I can lay down a road,
make wine that tastes good
and keep a factory smoking,
I go down to the depths of the earth
I conquer all the peaks,
I walk among the stars
and carve furrows all over the earth.

I learned the language
of my masters and bosses,
they killed me over and over
for daring to raise my voice,
but I get up off the ground again
helped by the hands of others,
for now I'm not alone,
now there are so many of us.

translated by Adrian Mitchell

Manifiesto

Yo no canto por cantar
ni por tener buena voz,
canto porque la guitarra
tiene sentido y razón.

Tiene corazón de tierra
y alas de palomita,
es como el agua bendita,
santigua glorias y penas.

Aquí se encajó mi canto,
como dijera Violeta,
guitarra trabajadora
con olor a primavera.

Que no es guitarra de ricos
ni cosa que se parezca,
mi canto es de los andamios
para alcanzar las estrellas.

Que el canto tiene sentido
cuando palpita en las venas
del que morirá cantando
las verdades verdaderas.

No las lisonjas fugaces
ni las famas extranjeras
sino el canto de una lonja
hasta el fondo de la tierra.

Ahí donde llega todo,
y donde todo comienza,
canto que ha sido valiente
siempre será canción nueva,
siempre será canción nueva.

(1972)

Manifesto

I don't sing for love of singing
or to show off my voice,
but for the statements
made by my honest guitar.

For its heart is of the earth
and like the dove it goes flying,
tenderly as holy water,
blessing the brave and the dying.

So my song has found a purpose,
as Violeta Parra would say,
yes, my guitar is a worker,
shining and smelling of spring.

My guitar is not for killers
greedy for money and power,
but for the people who labour
so that the future may flower.

For a song takes on meaning
when its own heart beat is strong
sung by a man who will die singing
truthfully singing his song.

I don't sing for adulation
or so that strangers may weep
I sing for a far strip of country
narrow but endlessly deep.

In the earth in which we begin,
in the earth in which we end,
brave songs will give birth
to a song which will always be new,
to a song which will always be new.

translated by Adrian Mitchell

Cuando voy al trabajo

Cuando voy al trabajo
pienso en ti,
por las calles del barrio
pienso en ti,
cuando miro los rostros
tras el vidrio empañado,
sin saber quiénes son, donde van …
pienso en ti,
mi vida, pienso en ti.
En ti, compañera de mis días
y del porvenir,
de las horas amargas y la dicha
de poder vivir,
laborando el comienzo de una historia
sin saber el fin.

Cuando el turno termina
y la tarde va
estirando su sombra
por el tijeral,
y al volver de la obra,
discutiendo entre amigos,
razonando cuestiones
de este tiempo y destino…
pienso en ti,
mi vida, pienso en ti.
En ti, compañera de mis días
y del porvenir,
de las horas amargas y la dicha
de poder vivir,
laborando el comienzo de una historia
sin saber el fin.

On My Way to Work

On my way to work
I think of you,
through the streets of the town
I think of you,
when I look at the faces
through steamy windows
not knowing who they are, where they go…
I think of you
my love, I think of you.
Of you, compañera of my life
and of the future
of the bitter hours and the happiness
of being able to live,
working at the beginning of a story
without knowing the end.

When the day's work is over
and the evening comes
lengthening its shadow
over the roofs we have made,
and returning from our labour,
discussing among friends,
reasoning out things
of this time and destiny...
I think of you
my love, I think of you.
Of you, *compañera* of my life
and of the future,
of the bitter hours and the happiness
of being able to live,
working at the beginning of a story
without knowing the end.

Cuando llego a la casa
estás ahí
y amarramos los sueños…
laborando el comienzo de una historia
sin saber el fin.

(1973)

When I come home
you are there
and we weave our dreams together…
working at the beginning of a story
without knowing the end.

translated by Joan Jara

Estadio Chile

Somos cinco mil
en esta pequeña parte de la ciudad.
Somos cinco mil.
¿Cuántos seremos en total
en las cuidades y en todo el país?
Sólo aqui, diez mil manos que siembran
y hacen andar las fábricas.

¡Cuánta humanidad
con hambre, frio, pánico, dolor,
presión moral, terror y locura!

Seis de los nuestros se perdieron
en el espacio de las estrellas.

Un muerto, un golpeado como jamás crei
se podría golpear a un ser humano.
Los otros cuatro quisieron
quitarse todos los temores,
uno saltando al vacío,
otro golpeándose la cabeza contra el muro,
pero todos con la mirada fija de la muerte.
¡Qué espanto causa el rostro del fascismo!
Llevan a cabo sus planes con precision artera.
Sin importarles nada.
La sangre para ellos son medallas.
La matanza es un acto de heroísmo.
¿Es éste el mundo que creaste, Dios mio?
¿Para esto tus siete días de asombro y de trabajo?

En estas cuatro murallas solo existe
un número que no progresa,
que lentamente querrá más la muerte.

Pero de pronto me golpea la conciencia
y veo esta marea sin latido,
pero con el pulso de las máquinas
Y los militares mostrando su rostro
de matrona lleno de dulzura.

Chile Stadium

There are five thousand of us here
in this small part of the city
We are five thousand
I wonder how many we are in all
in the cities and in the whole country?
Here alone are ten thousand hands which plant seeds
and make the factories run.

How much humanity
exposed to hunger, cold, pain,
moral pressure, terror and insanity?

Six of us were lost
as if into starry space.

One dead, another beaten as I could never have believed
a human being can be beaten.
The other four wanted
to end their terror
one jumping into nothingness,
another beating his head against a wall,
but all with the fixed look of death.
What horror the face of fascism creates!
They carry out their plans with knife-like precision.
Nothing matters to them.
To them, blood equals medals,
Slaughter is an act of heroism.
Oh, God, is this the world that you created,
For this your seven days of wonder and work?

Within these four walls only a number exists
which does not progress,
which slowly will wish more and more for death.

But suddenly my conscience awakes
and I see that this tide has no heartbeat,
only the pulse of machines
and the military, showing their midwives faces
full of sweetness.

¿Y México, Cuba y el mundo?
¡Que griten esta ignominia!

Somos diez mil manos menos
que no producen.
¿Cuántos somos en toda la patria?

La sangre del compañero Presidente
golpea más fuerte que bombas y metrallas.
Asi golpeará nuestro puño nuevamente.

¡Canto que mal me sales
cuando tengo que cantar espanto!
Espanto como el que vivo,
como el que muero, espanto.
De verme entre tantos y tantos
momentos del infinito
en que el silencio y el grito
son las metas de este canto.
Lo que veo nunca vi,
lo que he sentido y lo que siento
harán brotar el momento…

(1973)

Let Mexico, Cuba and the world
cry out against this atrocity!

We are ten thousand hands
which can produce nothing.
How many of us in the whole country?

The blood of our President, our compañero,
will strike with more strength than bombs and machine guns!
So will our fist strike again.

How hard is it to sing
when I must sing of horror!
Horror in which I am living,
horror in which I am dying.
To see myself among so much
and so many moments of infinity
in which silence and screams
are the end of my song.
What I see, I have never seen.
What I have felt and what I feel
will give birth to the moment…

translated by Joan Jara

Notes

Víctor Jara of Chile
This poem was first published by Adrian Mitchell in *The Apeman Cometh* (1975). It was later set to music and recorded by Arlo Guthrie on the album *Amigo* (1976).

El aparecido
Víctor wrote this song for Che Guevara (1928-1967) shortly before Guevara was killed in the Bolivian jungle.

Plegaría a un Labrador
Víctor entered this song in the First Festival of New Chilean Song, held at the Estadio Chile in 1969. It won joint first prize.

Preguntas por Puerto Montt
On 9 March 1970, Chilean police used tear-gas and machine-guns against unarmed peasants who were squatting on wasteground on the outskirts of the southern city of Puerto Montt. Eight peasants were killed and 60 were wounded. Pérez Zujovic was the Interior Minister responsible for ordering the attack. Four days later Víctor sang this song at a huge demonstration in Santiago called in protest of the massacre.

A Luis Emilio Recabarren
Luis Emilio Recabarren (1876-1924) was a founder member of the Chilean Communist Party. He was well-known for encouraging the use of theatre, poetry and song at political meetings.

El alma llena de banderas
Miguel-Angel Aguilera was a young Communist and a member of the Brigada Ramona Parra street artists' group. He was shot dead by a plainclothes policeman while attending a demonstration in Santiago in 1970. His funeral was attended by several hundred thousand people.

Ni chicha ni limoná
Chicha is a strong alcoholic drink fermented from grapes and drunk by peasants at harvest time. *Limoná* in colloquial Chilean speech suggests a watered-down imported version of lemonade. The song was addressed, after the election of Allende, to undecided elements of the Chilean middle class.

Manifiesto
Violeta Parra (1917-1967) was a Chilean songwriter and folklorist; she was a member of the Chilean Communist Party and a friend of Victor's.

Cuando voy al trabajo
In May 1973 a friend of Víctor's, a young building-worker called Roberto Ahumada, was killed by a sniper while attending a peaceful demonstration in Santiago.

Estadio Chile
Víctor wrote this poem sometime between 12 and 16 September 1973 in the Chile Stadium, where he was imprisoned, tortured and murdered by the security forces. According to the testimony of his fellow prisoners, only the last verse, 'Canto que mal me sales' was intended to be sung. Isabel Parra (daughter of Violeta) later sang these verses *a capella*, and her beautiful recording was played in the Act of Purification of the Chile Stadium in 1991.

Further Reading

Joan Jara, Víctor: *An Unfinished Song* (Jonathan Cape, 1983; new edition, Bloomsbury 1998)

Joan Jara and Adrian Mitchell, *Víctor Jara: His Life and Songs* (Elm Tree Books, 1976)

Claudio Acevedo, Rodolfo Norambuena *et al* (eds), *Víctor Jara: Obra Musical Completa* (Fundación Victor Jara, 1996)

A full list of Víctor Jara's recordings can be found at:
http://www.nuevacancion.net/víctor/

For more information about Víctor Jara and his work, see
http://www.fundacionvíctorjara.cl/

The Translators

Eduardo Embry fled Chile after the coup in 1973. Two collections of his poetry, *The Book of Tricks* and *Manuscripts that Water Erases* have been published in Chile and Venezuela. His translations of the Venezuelan poet Gustavo Pereira were published as *The Arrival of the Orchestra* (Smokestack, 2010). He lives in Southampton.

Martín Espada is a Puerto Rican poet from New York. He has published more than fifteen books as a poet, editor, essayist and translator, including *Crucifixion in the Plaza de Armas: Poems* (Smokestack, 2008). He teaches poetry at the University of Massachusetts.

John Green worked for many years as a television journalist in the GDR and later as a trade union officer in Britain. His books include *Engels: A Revolutionary Life, Ken Sprague: People's Artist* and (with Bruni de la Motte) *Stasi Hell or Workers' Paradise: Socialism in the German Democratic Republic*.

Joan Jara is a dancer and choreographer. She left Chile after the Pinochet coup and the murder of her husband, and returned to Britain. Today she runs the Víctor Jara Foundation in Santiago, Chile.

Adrian Mitchell (1932-2008) was a poet, novelist, playwright and peace campaigner who believed in the power of poetry and song to change the world. Joan Jara and her two daughters stayed with Adrian and Celia Mitchell when they first arrived in London in 1973.